Learning to Live after Loss

Dale Tavares

Learning to Live after Loss
ISBN: Softcover 978-1-955581-98-1
Copyright © 2022 by Dale Tavares

All rights reserved. No part of this book may be reproduced or transmitted in any form or by any means, electronic or mechanical, including photocopying, recording, or by any information storage and retrieval system, without permission in writing from the publisher.

Parson's Porch Books is an imprint of Parson's Porch *&* Company (PP*&*C) in Cleveland, Tennessee. PP*&*C is a self-funded charity which earns money by publishing books of noted authors, representing all genres. Its face and voice is **David Russell Tullock** (dtullock@parsonsporch.com).

Parson's Porch *&* Company *turns books into bread & milk* by sharing its profits with the poor.

www.parsonsporch.com

Learning to Live after Loss

Contents

Dedication 7

I'm Not a Writer 9

A Little about Me 11

Dreaded Call 14

Divine Intervention 23

What God Put's Together 25

Legacy Of Love 29

My Dad 35

Grief 39

Finding My Way 41

No Surprises 42

Reflection 44

Life Marches On 50

What Now? 52

Self-Medicating 54

The Unseen 57

About the Author 60

Dedication

This book is dedicated to my mother, Opal Nelson. And in loving memory of my Father, Jimmy Dale Nelson.

Also, I want to say a huge thanks to my family and friends for their support and input.

I am grateful to have you all in my life!

I'm Not a Writer

I am not a writer. And you can ask my friend Libby, I might have tried to convince myself numerous times that maybe I misunderstood God when he told me to write this. But time after time, He reminded me to get back to it. Sometimes through random Facebook posts or church services that were speaking just to me.

Once I finally realized that if God wants you to do something he will get you through it. I started to be prompted what to write- and the words came easy. As my pastor said recently when he was speaking about Paul I am writing with an inspired pen. God gives me the words to write, and I am just doing my best to obey him.

God first prompted me that he wanted me to write a book in October 2021. Back then what I thought the book was going to be about was what God puts together or the unbreakable bond of marriage. But it wasn't until after my dad passed that I understood it was living with loss. He was getting me prepared by thinking about married people whom death had separated. I wasn't prepared to know in October what January would bring to my life. That is the wonderful thing about God. God knows that we wouldn't be able to handle the whole plan all at once. I remember when I applied and got the Walmart store manager job. If I would have known going in that a year later (to the day) I would get the word that I was going to have to close the store, I'm not sure that I would have applied. And all the experiences that I had would have been lost. Our human minds aren't ready to see the big picture. We

have to learn to trust him even though we can't see the next steps. I will say it is getting easier for me.

Sometimes when things go wrong (according to my standards) I start to look for what God is doing and how he will use the situation. Everything that I have gone through in my life has been preparing me for today- God uses our past and all our experiences for his purposes. Don't limit what God can do because you limit what you can do. Trust, obey and do.

"The Lord is good, a refuge in times of trouble. He cares for those who trust in Him"- Nahum 1:7

A Little about Me

My given name was Dale Deniece Nelson. I am an only child of Jimmy Dale Nelson and Opal Mae (Bobo) Nelson. I was born in Ripley, Mississippi. Unlike the stereotype of most only children, I was not spoiled. I always was aware of things that others might not have been conscious of. You might say I was an old soul. Sometimes, I was too smart for my own good. We lived in the same house my whole life. My Mom still lives in this house. My Dad moved around a lot as a kid, and never wanted me to go through that. He never went to school much. Back then, working was seen as more important than going to school, especially in large families. As a kid, I could be found playing school in my little playhouse my dad built me. Back then I wanted to be a teacher. I was in a few advanced classes.

I always had good grades. I really loved school.

I had a few good friends growing up. I never needed to be around a lot of people or to be the center of attention.

I met my husband, Danny Tavares, shortly after my high school graduation. I met him while I was working at Walmart in Corinth, Mississippi. He wasn't supposed to even be there, he should have been in Florida. Obviously, God wanted to make sure we met. We dated for about a year before we were married. We have been married 26 years right now. We have 3 kids who are all blessings and gifts of God. We have 4 grandkids that are amazing. We love them so much! We have had many addresses over the years and as in any marriage many ups and downs, but we love each other and that makes it all worth it.

When my dad passed away, I was 46 years old, and Dad was 74 years old. Even though that seems like a lot of time, it really isn't. It is never enough. I feel blessed that I had such an amazing father. I think of others who lost their dad's when they were very young or some that never got to meet their dad. At least I have all those precious memories to go back to. I think when my time comes and I am no longer here, I want wonderful times and great memories for my kids, my grandkids my husband and all my friends to have to look back to. I want to make every day count. Enjoy the little things, as I can see now, they are the big things. A simple phone call, a hug, a stroll through the garden looking at all the wonderful things that my dad grew, those are the things that I long for now. My parents, Jimmy, and Opal Nelson, are simple people who enjoy simple things and taught me to appreciate and enjoy the small things. I am so blessed that I had my parents and that I grew up where I did in Walnut, Mississippi.

They taught me so many things. But most importantly they taught me to be honest, be kind and to respect people.

Figure 1. From left to right on couch Makayla, Brandon, Kalani, Abigail, David, Dale, Leilani, Keoni. In the floor Kaelin and Danny.

Dreaded Call

On Tuesday January 25, 2022, at around 8:15 in the morning I received a call while I was at work. My Mom was calling to tell me they were at Urgent Care and that they had just received the news that Dad had covid and double pneumonia. I can't fully describe the horrible sinking feeling that I felt.

The doctor had prescribed my dad 5 medicines and had added Dad to the list of people requesting monoclonal antibodies. He had also suggested that they go to the ER. I told my mom that I was headed to see them. This is a 6-hour trip. I immediately told my work that I was headed to Mississippi I was going to be receiving a service award from the commissioners at 9 am and would be leaving immediately after that. I called my husband and told him what was happening and that I needed the car and that I needed him to take care of my dog Finley because I had to go be with my parents. I ran home and grabbed my toothbrush, make-up bag and night clothes then jumped in the car.

This six-hour car ride was spent with me praying and crying and asking God to heal my Daddy. When I got to Mom and Dad's house my dad had a 102-degree temp and my mom couldn't get him to drink anything. I got him Tylenol and had him to drink some Gatorade. In addition to the 5 medicines prescribed for him, they told Mom to get him Vitamin D, Zink, Vitamin C and Vitamin B and to start taking them right way.

We got him to eat Tuesday night, and we all hung out in the living room. I ran to the local Walmart to get some soup for Dad and Mom needed minutes added to her phone plan. While I was there, I picked up Dad a couple of Hershey bars.

That night Mom and I laid hands on Dad and prayed for his healing. We were asking God for a miracle.

With Dad's underlining health conditions, covid was always a concern. We had all planned to sleep in the living room. Dad was going to sleep in his chair so he could stay upright and Mom and I each on a couch. At some point in the night, I told Dad if he would be more comfortable in his bed that they should do that. He and Mom moved to their room. I will tell you I didn't get a lot of sleep that night.

Wednesday morning, Mom and I got up before Dad. Mom was making breakfast when I woke up to grab some coffee. When Mom had breakfast ready, she went to wake him up. I will tell you he didn't look good. His color was off. He was very pale and seemed out of breath from trying to get dressed. We had him to sit and took his pulse/oxygen saturation. It was around 45 the first time. Then after he calmed down a bit, it was still only 77. I was very concerned with these numbers and decided to call Dad's doctor when his office opened to see if we would be able to get an oxygen tank to help supplement Dad's oxygen levels for when they dropped like that. I called and they encouraged me to take Dad to the ER as he had to be evaluated before they could prescribe him an oxygen tank.

We got all of Dad's medicines and headed in my car to the ER. Dad really didn't want to go but I think he knew it was probably best.

When we got to the ER, I got them in to check in and went to park the car. They would only let one of us back with Dad and Mom wanted me to go to make sure I voiced Dad's wishes and why we were there.

My dad had a hard time hearing, and he didn't have his hearing aids in. I got to spend a majority of the time with him in the Emergency room with Mom waiting in the lobby. I was texting her and sending her pictures and updates all along the way.

They had taken x-rays and let us know that they wanted to keep Dad at least over night to monitor his oxygen and start him on some Covid medicine that they hoped would help him. They let me know that we would not be able to accompany Dad upstairs to his room. I let them know that this would not be acceptable as he couldn't hear well, and he was a little apprehensive to be there anyway. They said I would need to request this exception with the hospital administrator, and I said that would be just fine.

The hospital administrator called Mom and told her that she could stay with him but that she would need to have all her medicines and clothes as once she got upstairs that she would not be allowed to come back if she left. Mom ran home and grabbed her clothes and medicines and was prepared to stay with Dad.

Somewhere around 7 they were going to move him to a room. We had a nurse friend that let my mom come back and we all three got to stay together in his room in the ER while they were getting things ready to move him. At that time, I didn't realize how special that time would be. I gave them both hugs and Dad said he wished I didn't have to go, and I told him that Mom was going to stay I was going to go to their house, and I was going to come back to take him home as soon as I could.

I cried all the way back to Mom and Dad's house. The whole rules with covid of not letting people stay with their loved ones is so heartbreaking. When I got to their house, in order to keep my mind occupied, I decided to clean.

Thursday Morning, Mom and I were talking on the phone and then I face timed them. Dad was feeling a little better. His appetite was up, and he seemed to be doing better. We were thinking that Friday he should be able to come home.

Thursday night, Dad took a turn for the worse and had an issue coughing up some blood. His breathing was becoming more labored, and they had to move him to ICU. They let Mom go with him.

Mom called me around 9PM. She was upset that they had to move him, and they had to put in a catheter. Up until this point, Dad was still in his jeans. Mom was feeling a bit helpless and called me and of course I was feeling the same. It's really hard when you are unable to be there even if just to comfort one another.

Mom called me again at 11. She was still very worried and upset. I was trying to encourage her. I told her that it would be ok, and I even tried to talk to a nurse to see exactly what was going on. Apparently, Dad had pulled out his catheter and they had to sedate him. His temperature was also up, so they removed some of his blankets. This was also bothering Mom as Dad would always get cold and if he ever got the chills it took him a while to recover. Mom was trying to prevent this. Mom called me back at 2 something Friday Morning. Dad seemed to be doing worse and they were having to keep him on low sedation to help him breathe deeply. I told Mom I was going to get up and shower and just head to the hospital even if all I could do was sit in the lobby. I figured at least I would be closer in case they needed me.

I showered and dressed and had made myself a cup of coffee. Mom called back. She said the doctor wanted to talk to me. I got on the phone and Dr. Pace introduced himself to me. Dr. Pace told me that Dad wasn't doing well. He told me that Dad wasn't going to survive this. This statement caught me off guard. I was still expecting to be able to go pick up Dad sometime soon. I asked Dr. Pace if I could come up there and be with Dad and Mom, and he said yes. When I got to the ER, Dr. Pace said I could head up.

I was in shock. My heart was breaking. I grabbed my purse and ran to the car. I called Danny to let him know what was happening and what Dr. Pace had said. I called Aunt Sandra to let her know so she could pass this info on to the rest of the family, as I was trying to keep them all updated on Dad's condition via text. I was crying so hard I am surprised I made it to the hospital.

I made it to the hospital in record time and ran up to see Dad. I met Mom in the lobby. They were doing something when I got there, adjusting his sensors or something I believe. I went in to see Dad and he was sedated. I let him know I was there and that I loved him.

Shortly after I got there, they wanted to do an additional x-ray to see how Dad's lungs were looking.

Mom and I stepped into the hallway so they could do the x-ray. Mom and I didn't say a lot but we both were feeling the same way. Helpless.

Mom and I got to go back in, and Dad was still sedated. I sat and held one hand and Mom was holding his other. We were praying for a miracle. Complete healing.

When the results from the X-rays got back Dr. Pace came to show us. I always let Dad know what I was doing so I leaned down in his ear and said, "Dad, Mom and I are going to step out to look at your x- ray results." In that Moment, Dad opened his eyes for the first time since I was there. I said "Hi"- He said, "I didn't know you were here." I said, "I have been here for a few hours and Mom has been with you the whole time." He said they wouldn't let him sit up (they had his arms held down so that he didn't accidently pull out his catheter again).

Dr. Pace took turns showing us the results so that one of us could be with Dad while he was awake. He told us that Dad's lungs had deteriorated over the last 2 days since he got to the Hospital. His lung capacity was only partial in both lobes. He shared with us that even if we put him on a ventilator that it would not be enough to save his life. Dad had told both of us and even the nurse that he didn't want to be on a ventilator anyway. But I can tell you that if Dr. Pace would have said that would have saved his life, I would have wanted to try it. He told us we had some tough decisions to make. He said that if we were not going to put him on a ventilator then we needed to add the do not resuscitate because we would just be bringing him back to suffer. Mom and I discussed the fact we did not want him to suffer and that we did not want to get in God's way if it was Dad's time.

Dr Pace's shift was ending, and he told Mom and I to decide what we wanted to do. We had decided what we wanted to do, but we hadn't formally told this to anyone. I will tell you I was still praying for a miracle. I was not ready to give up my Daddy and I know God can do all things. We had put the blanket on Dad and the new doctor on the floor came in and said we were hindering them lowering Dad's temp- which was hovering at 103 pretty much the whole time since I got there. We shared with him Dad's condition and then he had asked us what we wanted to do. He ended up praying with me and Mom and later on was the one to pronounce Dad. We both got to be with Dad until he went home to be with Jesus at about 10 minutes till 1. They actually pronounced Dead at 12:58. We held Dad's hand the whole time.

Mom and I went home to sleep once the hospital got all the information they needed.

That next day, Saturday, we went to the funeral home to plan Dad's service. Visitation was on Monday night and Dad's funeral was on Tuesday. Tuesday was a rainy and chilly day until time for Dad's outside service, and then it was so sunny and warm. It was very much a God thing. The service was so beautiful.

There were some photos taken of the great grandbaby Keoni during this time. There were some pretty amazing sun rays that followed him and moved with him. There were also some orbs by him. I truly believe that was Dad's spirit there with us this day.

Sometimes people donate Bibles instead of flowers at funerals. My Dad had 107 Bibles donated in his name. He would be so happy that there are 107 Bibles that will hopefully lead others to Jesus.

Divine Intervention

I am so very glad that I took Mom and Dad to Mayberry in June 2021 and then threw them a 50th wedding anniversary party September 2021. This time spent with them will be with me forever. I just felt like I had to do both. Now I understand why. We are not promised a tomorrow- live each day as if it were your last. And now I know why God put in me such an urgency to make sure these things happened when they did, because we wouldn't get another opportunity. If God puts something in your heart and mind, do it! Don't question or try to talk yourself out of it. It might be the only opportunity you get.

I am a fixer. Sitting next to my dad in the hospital and not being able to do anything to help him was the worst feeling that I have ever felt. I wanted to just scream. But as my dad was getting closer to passing, I had a peace come over me, and Dad had a smile on his face when he went to be with Jesus.

I had so many thoughts going through my head like: would he still be here if I didn't take him to the ER- would he have gotten better at home? But I was reassured by the Doctor that it would have happened quicker at home without him being on oxygen- I am glad that Mom waited till I got there to take him to the ER. Otherwise, I would not have been able to stay with him. And without my requesting it from the hospital administrator, Mom would not have been able to stay with him. With Dad's hearing issues and his apprehension to even be at the hospital, I can see now how God worked all of this out.

We had some good times on Tuesday and Wednesday. And Mom and Dad had some special times together on Wednesday and Thursday before Dad got bad. I know she will forever be appreciative of those final days. And the fact that both of us got to be with him on Friday morning until he passed, during a time when no one is allowed to be, I can tell you I know that this is a God thing! God knew what Mom and I would need to be able to look back to. Sometimes it takes God's love to quiet us- Zephaniah 3:17

What God Put's Together

What God puts together is never really separated. Even by death. My parents got married in the year 1971. My Dad, Jimmy Dale Nelson was 23years old and my mom, Opal Mae Bobo was 19. Times were very different back then. People were more relaxed. Things were Simple, less complicated. September 14, 2021, my parents were married for 50 years.

My parents met when my mom was 11 years old. Dad was friends with my mom's older brother Raybon. They pretty much grew up together. Dad would come over to hang out with my mom's brother, Raybon, and stay and eat with them sometimes. When my mom was 14 years old, they started dating.

Five years later they were married. When I asked my mom how they met, she said their families just kinda hung out together and she knew in her heart that Dad was the one that God had for her.

Dad and Mom built the house I grew up in with their own hands. My Mom still lives there today. It wasn't built all at once. As they could afford to, they would continue to add on additional rooms.

My Dad worked for many years at Mr. Claude Wilbanks' sawmill and later on at Bass's sawmill. My dad was responsible for tripping the saw and running the edger. Tow jobs in one. A job that is super tough but that he loved so much.

My Mom said that God wasn't always a big part of their lives but that they always knew that they needed to do better. Seeds were planted by her stepsister Esba Crum. She said God used near miss accidents to remind them that they weren't on the right paths. My Mom said that she felt the secret to a long marriage is respecting one another and unconditional love. Talk your partner up to others and not down.

My Mom misses the fellowship she had with my dad. She remembers the wonderful times in their lives, like when I was born. She also remembers when their grandkids and great grandkids were born and how happy they were. Mom said she also remembers all the regular days in between that they shared.

I think grief is so much harder for people who have spent so much time together. People that have been married a substantial amount of time seem to have the most change during the loss of their spouse.

Everything reminds you of the other and you miss so much of just the little things that make up a life together. There are so many day-to-day activities that Mom misses, like watching Wheel of Fortune and every time they showed the island-hopping island my dad always joked because the island appeared so small, he always talked about not sticking your toe off. I have noticed that my mom says that now every time we watch Wheel of Fortune. And every time she does it makes me smile. My Dad is still with us. Maybe not in body, but in all of his jokes, in the songs that he would randomly burst out singing and all the things that he instilled in us. The happiness that he brought to our lives will never go away. Dad's faith also is still with us. There are many things that I remember, but one time Dad prayed for rain, and it rained not more than a few minutes later. Also, one time I remember a story where Dad was low on money and he needed something, and he was sitting in the car at Walmart as my mom went in. It was raining and he saw a twenty-dollar bill floating by the car. He used that to go into the store and get what he needed. Dad knew it was a God thing. Dad's faith builds my faith.

My Dad loved my mom and I got to watch them and learn from them about what love and a marriage should look like. Not always one hundred percent perfect, but always worth it. My Mom and Dad were married for 50 years and if God hadn't called him home, I'm sure they would have been together 50 more. They loved each other fiercely. I know not everyone had that security that I had, and I am very thankful for it. I am so glad that I got to witness this. Historically, I have had so many beautiful examples in my family of what a marriage should look like. It is wonderful to see marriages that hold the test of time.

Figure 2. Jimmy and Opal Nelson's 50th wedding anniversary

Legacy Of Love

I have had so many examples of what a great marriage looks like in my life. I have to warn you the next paragraph will remind you of the 139 verses from Genesis, the "begats" that everyone skips in the Bible. I believe those scriptures are important to show the lineage of Jesus. I believe the following is necessary to fully convey where I received my views on marriage. I see marriage as a sacred and holy union based on the dedication, loyalty, and length of time of these great marriages that I got to witness throughout my life.

My Grandparents were married for 58 years before Papaw Nelson passed. They were so very cute together and had such respect for each other. My Aunt Brenda and Uncle Charles have been married for 53 years. I can't even imagine one without the other. My parents were married for 50 years before my dad passed. Mom and Dad were perfect for each other. My mother and father- in- law have almost been married for 50 years. March 31, 2023, will be their anniversary. There is a lot of love between them.

My Aunt Helen was married to my Uncle Tony for 47 years before he passed. My Aunt Helen talked with me about the things that she misses since Uncle Tony's passing. I can tell you the things she spoke of are the small things, everyday things that make up a life together. My Cousin Gail and her husband Charles have been married for 47 years. They still enjoy spending all their time together. My Aunt Ann and my Uncle Vester were married for 42 years before my uncle Vester passed. They had a wonderful relationship. My Uncle Vester could always lighten up the mood. My Aunt Deb and my Uncle Raybon were married for 41 years before Aunt Deb passed. These two were the perfect couple. I know my uncle was heartbroken after her passing. She was his other half. Uncle Terry and Aunt Sherry were married 41 years before Uncle Terry passed. Uncle Terry had a great sense of humor, and he loved Aunt Sherry very much. My Aunt Judy and Uncle Levoyd were married for 35 years before my Aunt Judy passed. You could tell these two loved each other. My Aunt Lenda and Uncle Richard were married for 34 years before Uncle Richard passed. My Uncle Richard was a very wonderful man. He loved my Aunt Lenda something fierce. I know she had a huge hole in her heart when he passed. My cousin Karen and her husband David have been married for 33 years so far and still going strong. If you spend any time around them, you can see the love they have for each other. My cousin Becky and her husband William have been married for 33 years. These two complete each other. They both like to spoil one another.

My cousin Amy and her husband Tim have been married for 32 years. These two love to be with each other and share the love of exploring. My cousin Anthony and his wife Kelly have been married for 32 years so far. I can't remember a time when they were not together. My husband Danny and I have been married 26 years. We were married August 31, 1996. When I met him, I just knew he was the one. I remember having a conversation with my mom that he was the one. 26 years later, I still feel that way! My sister- in- law Shawna and brother- in- law Brandon just celebrated 25 years. These two were high school sweethearts. I can't imagine these two not together. It is so comforting for me to know that the wedding vows these folks have taken especially the till death do us part really meant that to them.

1 Corinthians 13:4-5 says" Love is patient, love is kind. It does not boast. It is not proud. It does not dishonor others. It is not self-seeking. It is not easily angered. It keeps no record of wrongs. "

I will tell you there is not one of those couples that would say that those words always described their marriage. But there is really something amazing when two people get it right. It is very inspiring. It just makes you feel good, like it's the way God intended. Marriage has always been sacred. And those vows should not be taken lightly. The actual vows from our ceremony aren't from the bible but are based on biblical principles. According to Genesis 2:24, the Bible defines marriage as the joining of two into one.

To have and to hold refers to the physical embrace of husband and wife, to have is to receive without reservation the total self-gift of the other. It is not a statement of ownership but a promise of unconditional acceptance. But relationships need to be nurtured. God's plan is to keep him as the center of the celebration of love. Sin can distort a perfect love story. But remember when trouble seems to brew there is only one that can solve it all, God. The last part of the vows says those whom God has put together let no man put asunder. When I read that it assures me that even though they might be physically separated here on earth by death, they are still one and connected. My Mom said something that got me to thinking - she said God wouldn't put families together to only separate them. She is a smart lady. And I know there is a whole spiritual realm that we are unaware of, but it is nonetheless real.

I had a dream not long after my dad passed, and he was talking to me in my dream about changing the scripture on the back of the bathroom door in my mom's house. It was a very real feeling dream, and I made note of it in my journal. I didn't remember there being a scripture located on the back of the bathroom door in Mom's house, but I intended to look the next time I went to visit.

When I went to visit, I looked on the back of the bathroom door and there was no scripture. I chalked it up to it being just a dream. That night there was a noise in the bedroom I was sleeping in. I heard the noise, woke up and didn't really know what it was, so I went back to sleep. This bedroom is attached to the bathroom from my dream. In the morning, Mom came in to wake me up and she said, "When did this fall?" There was a plaque of a Bible with a scripture that was hanging over Mom's door in the bedroom where I was sleeping. It had apparently fallen and was the noise I had heard in the middle of the night. I asked Mom what scripture it was, and I pulled out my journal and it was the very same scripture from my dream. I am not sure what all this means. In that moment I was shocked and comforted! It felt like a communication from my dad letting me know everything was ok. The scripture on the plaque was from John 14: 1-3 "Let not your heart be troubled; ye believe in God, believe also in me. In my father's house are many mansions: if it were not so, I would have told you. I go to prepare a place for you. And if I go and prepare a place for you, I will come again, and receive you unto myself; that where I am, there ye may be also. "

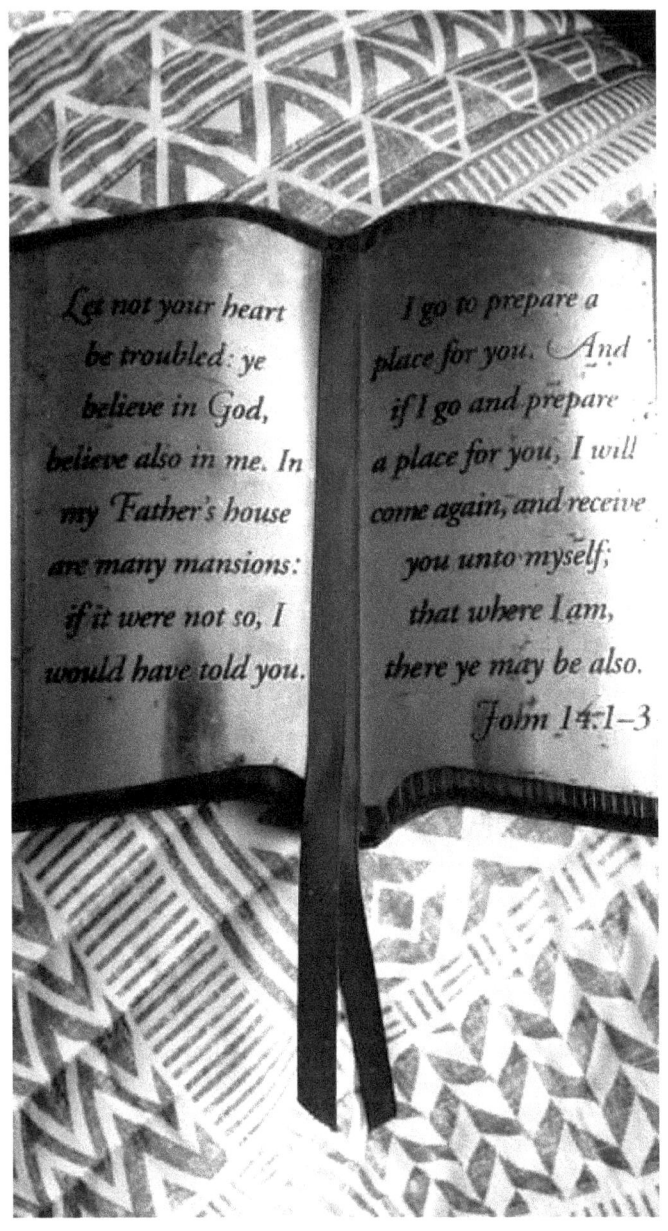

My Dad

There are so many wonderful things I could say about my dad. Even before my dad came to know Jesus, he was a good and moral man. As a matter of fact, that was one of the reasons why it took him just a little longer to come to know Jesus. Sometimes people that are morally good, look at Christians and say,

"Well, I am as good as they are." (Which is one of the sure ways to know that you aren't saved). When you come to Jesus, you understand that all your good is as filthy rags without Jesus. (Isaiah 64:6). We have all sinned and Romans 3:10 says "As it is written, there is no one righteous, not even one," My Dad was a quiet man, soft spoken and soft hearted. Even the end of King Kong, where you can hear the heartbeat, was too much for my Daddy. Sometimes you could tell he was just processing what everyone was saying. Lots of our phone conversations were about the weather or my garden or the kids. I could always hear so much in what he didn't say. My Dad loved his garden. He got great joy out of his prize tomatoes or cabbage. He didn't actually win any contests but there was always a competition between him and my Uncles Kenny and my Uncle Raybon. He loved to get the first tomato of the group. My Mom has and has sent me many pictures of him holding huge tomatoes or standing by his cabbages. That love of the garden and growing things rubbed off on me. There is just something about watching your plants grow and produce. I think God feels his way about us. He references these many times in His word. By their fruit ye shall know them-Matthew 7:16-20 KJV says 16 "Ye shall know them by their fruits. Do men gather grapes of thorns, or figs of thistles? 17 Even so every good tree bringeth forth good fruit but a corrupt tree bringeth forth evil fruit. 18 a good tree cannot bring forth evil fruit Neither can a corrupt tree bring forth good fruit. 19 Every tree that bringeth not forth good fruit is hewn down and cast into the fire. 20 wherefore by their fruits ye shall know them."

My Dad loved a good western or a nature show. He loved to hunt- not just for sport -but he loved deer meat. He was a country boy through and through. My Dad was wise-not because he had a fancy degree. Truth be told, I think my dad actually only had a 3rd grade education. Living made him wise. He listened to people, especially those older than him who had lived through stuff. That is the problem with the world today. Everyone wants a degree but the pass downs from our elders are not being absorbed. So many valuable life lessons are being forgotten. My Dad put other's needs ahead of his. Actually, some of the last things that he said to me, and my mom is that he didn't want us to get sick and catch what he had. That is the heart of a man that loved others more than himself. My Dad was a hard worker. Majority of his life he was a sawmill worker. It wasn't some glamorous job that everyone aspires to do. It was a hard day's work for little pay most days. But he loved it. He was creating something necessary for life and necessary to build. I think about Jesus. A carpenter's son. And scripture speaks of him being a carpenter too. Mark 6:3 "IS not this the carpenter son of Mary, Brother of James and Joses and Judas and Simon and are not his sister's here with us? And they took offenses at him." To think of the Son of God, anything that God could have imagined, and he made him one who builds who creates with a man's hands. There is something special indeed about growing and creating things.

My Dad loved his church and the people in it. He had so much respect and love for them. Dad was a deacon at Bethlehem Baptist Church. I remember his swearing in ceremony. I was so very proud of him.

He also enjoyed cooking at the church brotherhood breakfast. And I heard stories about him frying the best chicken and fish.

I love hearing the stories of my dad being a part of the church. It was a big part of him. I never heard my dad pray out loud, other than to ask grace over a meal. I know my dad prayed often. I know his prayers touched Heaven. I know he has called on God for many things and they were answered. I always said God loved my dad just a little more. He was genuine, never putting on airs. Reminds me a little of Elijah

James 5:16 says "Confess your faults to one another and pray one for another that ye may be healed. The effectual fervent prayer of a righteous man availeth much." Not only was Elijah a man just like my dad, with the same weaknesses as a man, but when he prayed, he prayed earnestly and with sincerity as just a man that believes in the power of his God. My Dad didn't like when I said that he was loved more. He didn't want anything to be put on him but all the glory to God.

My Dad loved his family. He loved his grand kids and great grandkids. They brought him so much joy. I know my dad loved me. He told me often, but he showed me more. I had a great childhood. I have no complaints. I know not everyone can say that. Not everyone had love and acceptance growing up, and my heart goes out to them.

Figure 3. Jimmy Nelson and Dale Tavares.

Grief

Grief is a very real and a very weird thing. It strikes for me in the weirdest of places and the strangest of times. In the quiet time in the middle of the night, standing in the yard letting Finley, my little white malte-poo dog, go potty. It also hits me in the quiet time in the shower. When I awake in the middle of the night, I replay every last conversation that took place between January 25th and Friday January 28th. It happens and it continues to happen over and over every time you close your eyes- you relive every last moment. I know with me when I re-live these moments, the human part of me says, "what if I did this, what if I did that." I rehearse all the should have and could haves- Would Dad still be here if I did this? Or that? Then my heart kicks in and reminds me that God makes no mistakes. Not one thing happens to us without God knowing. No one goes before their appointed time. I am so glad of the time I got to spend with my dad at the end. I am so thankful for the turn of events and how they played out. I see God in every one of the events and how they transpired. I still miss my dad like crazy. I am brokenhearted for my mother and for my kids and grandkids that they don't have more time to spend with him. He was a great man and I do believe that God does love my dad a little bit more than everyone else.

Losing someone you love is hard. You will have good days and bad days. Some days you will just seem to be happy even though there is no specific reason- other days you will feel sad for no reason at all. The key that I have found is to feel every emotion. It's okay to not be okay. Sometimes only when you fully embrace every emotion honestly can you truly begin to heal.

For those of us that have put our faith in Jesus Christ, we know that our family member or friend is in a better place. Even though, that loss and missing them is still very real.

Everyone deals with loss differently. One of the most important things is to not shut people out. Stay involved in family and friend's lives.

Keep memories of your loved one alive by speaking of them often. I think a lot of people try to avoid mentioning the person as not to remind the person or make them sad, but we remember and are sad anyway. Hearing stories or memories of our loved ones makes them feel still a part of our lives. I know I love to hear stories of my dad and I like to remember things that he said or did.

Finding My Way

The last 4 days that I was in Mississippi because of Dad's sickness replay over and over in my mind. While there are so many things I would have done differently- there are so many things that I am so very glad happened the way they did. I see God's hand on so many things those days. I couldn't fully see it then but now I understand. There are many other things I can't wait to see what happens as a result of my dad's sickness. My Dad see's it now. I know that one hundred percent for certain.

"I see your heart in all you do"- a person at my work said this statement to me. She doesn't even know how much that statement means to me. I pray daily for Jesus to use me for the world to see Jesus' love through me. I fail him so much with this. But I want people to see something different in me and to know that it is Jesus and him alone that makes anything about me seem different. If there is anything good in me, it is because of Jesus' love. "Every good gift and every perfect gift are from above…" James 1:17.

There is so much evil in the world today. So much violence and meanness everywhere you look. I don't know how people continue to get up every day without Jesus in their lives. For me it is everything.

No Surprises

During horrific events that happen, I have heard people say that they don't know why God would allow such things to happen or they ask why does bad things happen to good people? Trust me. The human part of me questioned why my dad wasn't healed. I can say it was not for a lack of prayer and faith and so much love. Then my spiritual heart said, "Dale there are no surprises to God. "He knew exactly when my dad would be taking his last breath. Everything that happened was just as it should have been. Did it hurt any less? No. There are times I still wake up and think, "If only I" - then the Holy Spirit inside me calms my mind- Sometimes it takes God's love to quiet us.

Zephaniah 3:17-18

17 The Lord Thy God in all the midst of thee is mighty; he will save he will rejoice over thee with joy; he

will rest in his love, he will joy over thee with singing. 18 I will gather them that are sorrowful for the

solemn assembly who are of thee to whom the reproach of it was a burden

My pastor spoke in church that there are some things we won't know the answers to until we get to Heaven. Some moments we won't fully understand how God used them for His good until we see him face to face.

His plans are greater than our plans and his ways are greater than our ways. Nothing surprises God. There is nothing that happens that hasn't gone through God first.

When I stop to think about this, it makes me smile - My Dad wasn't just another Covid death, God had a plan for my Daddy. He is using him even now to draw people to him. My Dad's life and love for Jesus speaks for itself.

Why do good things happen to bad people and bad things happen to good people? Why would God allow this? Nothing surprises God. Nothing happens to any of us without it first going through God- My pastor said this morning "God uses things from our past, for his purpose in the future."

Some things we won't understand this side of Heaven- the choice to heal some and not heal others- God's plan is so much better than ours, His ways are better than ours. We may not see the full picture until we get to Heaven.

God doesn't take someone even a minute before it is their time. Hearing stories of what others are going through solidifies the faith of some. He uses all things for the good of those that love him.

Reflection

When you lose someone, you love, I believe God gifts us all for a time with reflection. Times gone by; we remember great memories but also start to see what we want our legacy to be. How we want those that we love to think of us. My thought is that he only gives us this for a short time and, if we don't grasp it, it fades away. Otherwise, all of us would live each day to the fullest, be the best version of ourselves we could be.

This would include never being angry or letting a harsh word be said without an apology. But like many of God's gifts, if we don't use them, we lose them, or they slip away. I hope I never take life for granted again. I hope that my life screams how much I love my family and friends and just how much they mean to me. I hope no one ever has a doubt about my feelings toward them. I don't want to be lacking when my time comes. I want to know that I used my time here wisely and with purpose to lead others to Jesus, and to be a witness of his love.

I want to continue to love to hear the birds chirping even at 3 am when I am taking the dogs potty. I hope to be amazed at all the stars at midnight when I am taking the dogs outside. (I just realized that a lot of my amazement and reflection happens at the least opportune times when everyone else is sleeping and the world is peaceful and quiet). I love walking around in the morning while it is still early, having coffee and looking at all my plants and my garden. It is such a peaceful time.

Very few things bring me as much joy as growing a garden. There is just something so satisfying about growing your own food and growing beautiful flowers.

I acquired this love from my father. Oh, how he loved to garden. It was a labor of love for him, and he loved to get the biggest and the first tomatoes. I always loved having Mom send me pictures of him with his prize tomatoes or his cabbages. He would always grow some huge ones. Dad never complained about all that it took to get it all ready. He truly enjoyed it. I have found gardening is a form of therapy it for me. Not only is gardening a relaxing thing for me but reminds me of my dad. I still have some green onions that he gave me that continue to come back year after year. Just today while staking my tomatoes I thought of how proud he would be to see me doing that. He loved to talk to others about his garden.

Figure 4. Jimmy Nelson prepping his plants.

Some other things my family likes to do in the evening is to sit out back by the fire pit. Sometimes the kids have friends over and we sit out back and roast hot dogs or marshmallows over the fire. This is so very peaceful for me.

Time is fleeting, ever changing. You never get it back. You can only appreciate it now, in the moment.

Cherish every bit you get with those you love. We are not promised a tomorrow. We never know when our time will be over. Sometimes I think "Would I really want to know when my last day would be?" I think that if I did, I would try to cram too much in and not really enjoy the little things, which make up the big things in our life. Some of my favorite little things are feeling the breeze on my face, the first touch of hot water on my shoulders in the shower, the feeling of the sunshine on my face, the first sip of coffee, the sound of a child laughing, excitement of Christmas morning as a child, riding the motorcycle in the country, reading a book on a rainy day snuggled up with a blanket on the couch, the smell of an old bookstore or the smell of a flea market, the excitement that you feel when you buy the perfect gift for someone and you know they will love it. I love creating something new with yarn, hugging a person that I love and having them really hug me back, giving someone, something knowing they can never return the favor. Holding my grandkids for the first time, Saturday morning cartoons as a child, snuggling with my dog, the feel of fresh sheets on my bed, the taste of buttery popcorn at the movies, sound of rain hitting a tin roof, watching the snowfall, and waking up to a winter wonderland. These things aren't on the list of monumental things as far as society goes, but for me they are everything. Don't get me wrong I enjoy holidays and special monumental things with my family too, but I think some of the ones I listed above are pretty important too for my wellbeing.

Other times I think I would like to know when my last day would be so that I could be absolutely sure that I did all I needed to do. I would start with living with purpose, on purpose, being present and making every last moment count.

I think God doesn't let us see the big picture, the whole plan because our simple human minds couldn't take the complexity. It would be too much for us.

I am ok with God being in charge of my life. I would totally make a mess of things. I am not too good at following directions even with baking. I certainly can't be trusted with huge important issues. I am glad that with his guidance I don't have to make them on my own.

When we lose someone or something God always gives us something. He never leaves us empty handed. It might be an unexpected friend or a new love or a new hobby. Have you ever heard the saying that when God closes a door, he opens a window? It is the same concept. Sometimes we don't realize it.

I know for me, the loss of my dad has made me closer to my aunts, uncles, and cousins, especially those on my dad's side of the family. It has also strengthened the bond my mom and I have. It has opened my eyes to how very precious life is and that we should take nothing for granted. For others who have lost a spouse or a life companion or friend, God may send you someone to fill that void. He might send you someone to share the rest of your days here on Earth with. God's plan for us is not to do this life alone.

For others he may give you a better job- like with me when my Walmart store was closed unexpectedly, he led me to the prosecutor's office which I absolutely love. I feel so rewarded now going to work every day. Still, others who have lost the ability to care for yourself, or lost a limb or your sight, God has or will gift you with a strength and resilience like you have never had before. Still others who have lost a friend or a child or a pet, God might reveal a purpose to you in your pain. It might not be easy but with God, you can make it through.

Life Marches On

When someone you love passes, the world feels like it should just stop. But it doesn't. Life just keeps on going. The days start and night comes one after the other. Everything just keeps right on happening.

I feel like those first few weeks I was just unplugged, going through the motions but not present. How could life keep going without my Daddy here? I couldn't imagine things continuing as they used to. I was so glad my work was closed a few extra days because of weather. I didn't want things to just keep on as if nothing had happened. I wanted to jump off the train of life and just be still, do nothing. God knew exactly what I needed and gave us a snowstorm. The white nothingness was just what I needed, to see the purity of the snow and the stillness. I needed to be lost in my thoughts with no responsibilities.

Sometimes, just time alone, sitting and not doing anything is exactly what you need to do. Truthfully, sometimes I would just sit and stare- no thoughts, no movement- just staring off into space. It takes your mind and heart longer to process the loss. Sometimes it means more to just be still, to just be. It's great therapy. Sometimes I don't know how or what I feel, but I always feel better just by being silent and still. My Dad has been gone a little over 6 months as I am writing this and there are still times now when I still need that. Eventually you gotta plug back in and understand you have to move on. It doesn't mean forgetting or loving them any less but being fully present and really feeling your emotions. Good days, bad days, blah days and really great days and there will be some of all of them. The living honors our loved ones by living and loving fully.

Remember, nothing can stop God's will from happening. No amount of prayer or love will hold or keep a person here on this earth if it is their time. Stop the what- if game. Can you out do or do better than God? No. Once we fully understand that God's ways are greater than our ways and His thoughts are greater than our thoughts, we can trust Him in His plan even when our hearts are breaking or are broken.

What Now?

We are all dealing with something. Yours might not be the loss of a family member but the loss of a friend, the loss of a job, a marriage, a pet, your freedom, or your home. It's been my experience that with any loss it takes great faith and courage to get back to it. I believe if God brings you to it, he will see you through it. Things might never be the same, but He will help you to begin again. It might not happen overnight, but it will happen. For those of us who are Believers we know that we will see our loved ones again. It is enough some days to just know that this life here is not the end. Everyone at some point and time will experience hard times. Those are the times when you decide what is going to be important to you. Material belongings are not everything. Even marriage and friendships don't define who you are.

You are so much more than your address, where you work or who you associate with. Your true worth is found in Jesus. You are what He says you are. Your purpose through him is so much greater than any title you could achieve here on Earth. God has a plan for your life and what you are going through today will be part of your testimony tomorrow. He will use your story to encourage someone else along the way. God loves you more than you can imagine. This one scripture always speaks volumes to me.

Psalm18: 16-19 MSG "But me he caught-reached all the way from the sky to the sea, he pulled me out of that ocean of hate, that enemy of chaos, the void in which I was drowning. They hit me when I was down, but God stuck by me. He stood me up on a wide- open field. I stood there saved- surprised to be loved. "

I miss my dad terribly and would love to see him, call him, or talk to him about the weather or his garden. But in my heart, I can carry on knowing that one day I will see him again. He will be waiting for me when I go home to Heaven.

Psalm 61:2: "When my heart is overwhelmed lead me to the rock that is higher than I."

Self-Medicating

That is the way my doctor described me when my contact prescription started to get a little off and I just began wearing only one contact.

But we do this all the time and sometimes it is not as harmless as wearing only one contact. It could be anything from overeating, drinking too much alcohol, disrespecting ourselves and not respecting our bodies- all with an effort to "see further."

What I have learned is that self-medicating just puts a band-aid on your issue. It really doesn't fix anything. It is just temporary.

In my situation, my eye prescription had gotten better in each eye which was why I couldn't see as well using my old contacts. But after my eye doctor, who is trained, got me a prescription to fit my needs, I can see better.

My point is that sometimes we need to consult with others to be able to see better. Don't try to go at it alone and self-medicate. Whatever self-medication you are using, whether it be alcohol, drugs, sex, or something else, remember, it is temporary. Talk to someone. Even if it is not a doctor or a counselor, find a friend and just share what all is going on. Sometimes just saying it out loud helps so much.

I have had many losses in my life from pets to grandparents, aunts, uncles, friends and most recently my dad. What I have learned is that you grieve them all differently. Each has their own place in your heart and there is no set right or wrong way to go about it.

My Dad has been gone since January 28, 2022. Yesterday was a sad day. I woke up that way. Nothing significant or special about the day, just my heart decided. With my friend Laura, it has been almost four years since her death. I will see her name on a case at work or read a note that she made and the

sadness returns. It is the same with grandparents, family members and pets. Something will trigger a memory and emotions come with that. We are all human. We are created to have connections with others. Those connections don't suddenly stop when that person or thing passes. The feelings are still there. Sometimes tied to a memory is a song, a smell, or an item of clothing. I often wear some of my dad's clothing. It makes me happy and feel closer to him.

Whatever helps you is what you should do. Grieving is personal. No manual or set of steps will work for everyone.

My faith is what I depend on. Last night my church was super helpful in helping my sadness. For me, my family and friends help to ease the pain. It is important to have a support group. Your support group can be made up of friends, family or maybe even strangers that all come together for the same purpose. It is super important that you have people that you can confide in and share your feeling with.

There will be sad days but also happy days. Take each day as it comes and live fully in the moment.

Remember to have no expectation of where you need to be by now. You are unique and so is your grieving process.

"I will not forget you! See, I have engraved you on the palms of My hands." - Isaiah 49:15-16

God's ways are greater than our ways! One day we will know and understand His wonderful and marvelous plan for our lives.

We know that God causes everything to work together for the good of those who love God and are called according to His purpose for them. Romans 8:28.

The Unseen

Have you ever walked outside at night and spotted a star? When you started to look closely at it then just like magic you start to see more stars? I think this is a perfect way to escribe life before Jesus.

Some things don't reveal themselves until we focus. They were always there - we just couldn't see them.

I pray this book brings comfort to you. I hope that in hearing my story you can see that you are not alone. I also pray that your relationship with Jesus is strengthened. If you don't have a relationship with Jesus, I pray that you come to know him. Salvation is a gift. It was paid for on the cross when Jesus Died for you and me.

"We have peace with God through our Lord Jesus Christ"- Romans 5:1

"For God so loved the world that he gave his one and only Son, that whoever believes in him should not perish but have eternal life" - John 3:16

"If you declare with your mouth, "Jesus is Lord," and believe in your heart that God raised him from the dead, you will be saved."- Romans 10:9

Here is how you can accept Christ into your life. Admit your need for a Savior. Turn from your sins.

Believe that Jesus Christ died for you on the cross and rose from the grave. Pray for Jesus to control your life through the Holy Spirit. You can pray the prayer below (or a similar prayer).

"Dear God, I admit that I am a sinner. I ask for your forgiveness. I believe Jesus is your son and He died for my sins. I believe you raised Him to life. I trust Him as my Lord and Savior. I ask for you to come into my heart and guide me and help me do your will. In Jesus name I pray. Amen "

If you prayed this prayer, I encourage you to share with a pastor that you have accepted Jesus. Get involved in a church and take the next steps and be baptized.

When my mom read my first rough draft, this was a note she wrote and tucked into my journal.

"Dale, I wanted you to know your words in this book have blessed me more than you could know. I am so glad you listened to God as He spoke to you about writing this. It means so much just to see your heart because we have been through this together. The loss of your dad breaks our heart. As we put our trust in God, He gives us peace. So thankful for you. I love you with all my heart" - MOM

As we go through the many changes and emotions that you feel with a loss, I pray this gets easier for all of us!

Remember: God is real. God loves you. He only wants the best for you.

"Pour out your hearts to Him, for God is our refuge."
- Psalm 62:8

About the Author

Dale Tavares is the mother of 3 amazing children: Makayla, Kalani and Leilani. She has been happily married to her husband Danny Tavares since August 31, 1996. She is a grandmother of 4 wonderful grand kids: David, Abigail, Keoni and Kaelin. She enjoys spending all her spare time with family and friends. She resides with her family in Ozark, Missouri.

www.ingramcontent.com/pod-product-compliance
Lightning Source LLC
Chambersburg PA
CBHW070656050426
42451CB00008B/373